THE BOOK OF WINTER CURES

◦ New And Selected Poems ◦

By Tony Curtis

Poetry

The Shifting Of Stones
Behind The Green Curtain
This Far North
Three Songs Of Home

Edited

As The Poet Said...

Plays

On Famine Road
 with Paul Goetzee and Jack Bradley

The Third Policeman by Flann O'Brien
 adapted with Jack Bradley

THE BOOK OF WINTER CURES

New And Selected Poems

Tony Curtis

Black Hills Press Poetry

Published in 2002
by Black Hills Press
Avalon,
Alma Park,
Monkstown Village
County Dublin,
Ireland.

All rights reserved. For permission
to reprint or broadcast these poems,
write to The Black Hills Press.

Copyright © Tony Curtis 2002

Designed and set in Adobe Garamond
by Pat Mooney
Printed and bound in Ireland
by Modus Media

ISBN 0-9544146-0-8

for Paula, Theo, Pat and Raffaela.

"Like it was written in my soul"
$$\text{Dylan}$$

Acknowledgements

The poems in this selection appeared in **The Shifting Of Stones** (Beaver Row Press 1986); **Behind The Green Curtain** (Beaver Row Press 1988); **This Far North** (Dedalus Press 1994) and **Three Songs Of Home** (Dedalus Press 1998). The new poems will be collected in the forthcoming book **What Darkness Covers.**

For the uncollected poems, acknowledgements are due to the editors of the following publications where some of these poems first appeared:
The Irish Times, Poetry Ireland Review, Portal (EXPO 2000) *Equinox, Force 10, The Irish Studies Review, Stinging Fly, The Bloomsday Magazine, An Tain (Melbourne) The Irish Journal (Perth) The Irish Scene (Perth).*

Many of these poems have been broadcast on *RTÉ, Lyric FM, Anna Livia,*

'Juliet Sleeping' appeared in *The Write Stuff — English & Media Studies for Transition Year.*

'Masterplan' appeared in *The Living Stream: a Festschrift for Theo Dorgan.*

'The Boat' appeared in *Out to Lunch* an anthology of Irish poetry sponsored by the Bank Of Ireland.

'Another Room' appeared in English and Flemish in *De Brakke Hond* (Belgium)

'Nude', 'Big' and 'Blind' appeared in the *Clifden Anthology*

'Currach' was set to music by the renowned Irish composer Ian Wilson.

This small selection is issued in Australia for my tour round the edges of that vast land.

    I would like to thank The Irish Arts Council for their generous assistance. Thanks are also due to Sheila Pratschke of The Tyrone Guthrie Centre at Annaghmakerrig and everyone at Varuna – The Writers' House granted by the Eleanor Dark Foundation. Their awarding of an Exchange Fellowship helped to make this long trip possible.

    A debt of gratitude is owed to Pat Mooney and David Curtis for all the time and effort they put into the shaping of this book; their advice and support were invaluable.

    First and last, I'd like to thank Mary and Oisin who where there as I made these poems. May God bless and keep them always.

CONTENTS

Redeemed 11

from **The Shifting Of Stones**

Home Thoughts 14
The Shifting Of Stones 16
The Morning After Eden 17
The Suitcase 18

from **Behind The Green Curtain**

The Touch 20
Behind The Green Curtain 22
Siren Off Inisheer 24
A Winter's Tale 25
On A Mountain Road 26

from **This Far North**

Penance 28
Preferences 29
The Dreaming 31
When Sometimes All I Can Imagine Are Hands 33
Unveiling 34
The Dowser And The Child 36
I Am The Night-Watch 38
Tea 40
The Coat 42
Northern Haiku 43

from **Three Songs Of Home**

Still Life 46
In Darjeeling 47
Prayer Guide 48

The Journey Home 49
Now That I Am Almost Dead... 51
A Habitable Place. 52
Blue Bowl 56
Lobsang's Last Wish 58
The Voyage 59
A Quiet House. 60

from **What Darkness Covers**

Blind 62
Juliet Sleeping. 63
Masterplan. 64
Still Life With Books 66
Nude 67
What Darkness Covers 69
Baffled 71
Jimmy 74
Lemon Tree 76
Small Interior. 77
Two Poems After Lucian Freud
   Big. 81
   Naked Girl With Egg. 83
The Olympians 84
Another Room 88
Now Winter's Over. 89
Currach. 90
The Boat 92
from The Book Of Winter Cures
   The Cure For A Broken Heart 93
   The Cure For Loneliness. 95

Redeemed

for Michael Hartnett

*After years in the quietest of rooms
I have taken to the road again.
God, in his wisdom,
has left everything unblessed:
the withering trees; the bracken
that covers the bones of winter;
the hawthorn, the blackthorn;
the stone walls gone to ruin;
the mongrel ditch, the culled fields.
I place myself amongst them
and feel at home.*

from The Shifting Of Stones

Home Thoughts

I was born in Dublin
between the docklands
and the Hill of Howth.
A Catholic's youth,
said prayers beside the quiet
alter of my little bed.
A Catholic's education —
the soft swish of leather
against the dark robes.

The clock ticking slowly
through classes in Irish and English;
I learnt the poetry of fear.
Lived for the summer months,
the holy days: Easter; Whit:
'Hail glorious Saint Patrick'.
Awaited the death of de Valera.
Through those school-days the taste
of freedom was always on my mind.

I remember the joy of being
called early from class to sing
soprano in the school choir.
Bored, I stood at the bottom
of a small squad of boys
gazing out as the clouds pushed past
towards Wexford, Galway, Donegal,
or perhaps, like the mailboat
I took, towards Holyhead.

Land of dead Kings and old Queens.
Land of Shakespeare, who saw through both

and reached into our soul.
Land of mad Cromwell, blind Milton.
Land of that epic idiot Spencer.
Did you know there's a Curtis in
'*The Taming of the Shrew*'?
An aged servant who dreams of better times,
and spends his days opening doors for others.
So many of the Irish in London,
myself included, unrehearsed,
could have played his role so well.

Seven years I spent in England.
I didn't then, nor do I now,
understand why I left these shores.
Though when I stand on a bog on such
an unholy day as this, knowing that every
wet shadow I meet along the road
is heading for shelter,
it's only natural to think,
that in my day Dublin was much like this —
a wilderness for childhood. In my youth
the world and its streets were cold.
That's my story.

The Shifting Of Stones

Old shipyards
like old women
wither and die;
too much water
in their bones.

Yet, when they
were young, their
still, quiet waters
offered safe harbours;
homes for weary bones.

The song and dance
of a salty sailor charmed
my mother. The sea rocked
against her sides,
calm until the storms.

Now the stones
have shifted,
the gantries rusted.
The blessing of ships
has not been heard for years.

The Morning After Eden

I was born old,
conjured out
of a cracked rib.

Your cold hands
bent me into this
peculiar shape.

I screamed
with pain.
I hated you.

Day after day,
your cold eyes
stared at my nakedness.

I ate your fucking apples,
ate until I was sick
and you dragged me away

by the hair.
Your parched laughter
has made you hoarse.

My body is sore
from your weight.
You have not bathed

since you were dirt.
Sleep can't take you away,
you are part of me.

The Suitcase

This is the Kilburn High Road
running up towards Cricklewood
away from England's Edgeware Road
where the homeless Irish come
carrying their father's battered suitcase,
though their father may have never left home.
They used to buy them at the summer fairs
for that day when their time would come,
or get them off a friend who died,
his lifelong journey finally done.
That's how my father stayed in his fields.
His suitcase travelled to him
from an Irish woman with a soft Kerry voice,
whose children's eyes were Irish blue
and accents East End Cockney.
She had married three times in England
and returned sadly widowed again.
The locals said "she deserved what she got
the saintless, unGodly woman."
Yet they listened discreetly to the stories she told
of how one husband left in a blitz of booze,
another in a blitz of bombs,
the last one dying on a beach outside Calais
his toes barely touching French soil.
She used to giggle at the thought,
said it reminded her of once
when he danced on Brighton beach
in nothing but his cotton drawers.
When she died the priest brought round her suitcase.
My father left it by the door.
In our kitchen someone was always leaving home.

from Behind The Green Curtain

The Touch

I

The West of Ireland is an empty church
built of curdled blood and brittle bone,
of sheep's placenta, flies, hedge, scutch.
Blessed are those who cross its graveyard of stone.
A while ago I saw the priest, a man of thirty
or forty, ambling across the back of the bog.
On a mission from God? No, he passed me
wearing a walkman, he was simply out walking his dog.
And I thought of my temptation on the Bog of Allen
that day with Mary Molly from outside Enniscorthy,
when no priest passed or came near the ditch.
As we stood naked, the last of our clothes fallen,
I heard a voice say "bogs never saw the like in Galway."
Surely, in all the world, that Eden had God's touch.

II

Shortly after I finished that poem
a farmer wandered into the back bar
of the Milestone and told me he was on to me.
He had seen me standing at his gate
with my pen and my bits of paper,
noting his crops, counting his sheep,
his cows, his fields. Leering at his wife.

"You, you're a land inspector. A whore
that lives on other men's misfortune."

"I'm not," says I, "I'm the bad end of a poet."

"God forgive you," says he, "a poet is it,
you and your kind have been a plague
on our country since blind Raftery
and Ó Brúadair took to the road
with their curses and their curious thoughts.
Damn you and your dirty books,
and your blind eyes that have never
seen the light inside a church."

I never met that man before,
nor have I seen him since.
Though often, I have felt his coldness
move over my grave and his spittle
run slowly down my headstone.

Behind The Green Curtin

That winter she froze
behind the green curtain.

Cold rose through her toes
into her bones. Her hair grew.

His hands caught her form.
His eyes the shadows on her skin.

Damp days folded one into another
until he coughed thin blood,

walked towards the light and heaved
up the great Georgian window,

taped shut for years against
the artist's fear of dust on oil.

Forgetting her nakedness she went
to take him from the open window.

He jumped. Blew his life out
as easily as he would a candle.

She leaned out, it was a red painting
he'd created with his life and broken bones.

A shopkeeper's eyes moved over
the white curves of her breasts.

Did he think them quarreling lovers?
Did he imagine a scented room,

tossed sheets on a tossed bed,
two white pillows,

clothes left where they had fallen,
a skirt covering a chair's modesty?

She walked slowly back across
the painter's room. Then wrapped

the green curtain over her bare shoulders,
feeling warm for the first time in days.

Siren Off Inisheer

A Japanese kimono seemed out of place
in the draughty three roomed cottage
sunk into the back of Inisheer, but
there you were, breasts tucked like
oranges in the colourful soft silk.

You arched your back and a shy ghost
lifted the kimono off your shoulders,
it slid to the floor and you were gone.
Through the small crucifixed window
I shivered as you plunged and surfaced

like a seal a few yards beyond the rocks.
Then I noticed the caps rising on the pier.
The eyes of the three women by the front wall.
I could hear your siren's call from the sea.
I lifted your kimono and the latch off the door.

A Winter's Tale

The road led up off over the mountains,
stopping at the village with a pond
that no one ever painted, but was like
those you see in landscape paintings.

They stopped the car. Ordered two pints.
Thick cream flowed from the heads down
onto the wooden counter. They drank.
Buttoned their coats when leaving.

The smell of beer was on their breath
as they pushed through the half-door
upsetting a child's tricycle. Plates
splintered as the woman hit the floor.

They left by the back door. Taking shirts
off the line to wipe the blood from their hands.

On a Mountain Road

for Oisin

The first fall of snow has frozen
the earth white as a dead man's hand.
From where I stand on this lonely bog
they call the feather bed, to the
curve in the road, between the grotto
and the graveyard, at quiet Glencree,
the sky is gone. So too the mountains
with their patchwork of hawthorns
that quilts the land into fields.
Rivers remain. Somewhere salmon leap
to catch the white flies before they
melt on the river's wet back. Sheep die.

I have brought my small son out
to creature this white wilderness
with the memory of our footprints,
the dark shadow of our shades.
His small hand steadies my step.
His eyes, slit like a hawk's, scan.
He tells me all he sees. Thinks he sees.
A cloud, is smoke drifting from the hostel
at Glencree; a bag caught on a fence,
someone waving in the distance. He waves.
Awakening in me forgotten memories.
Kindling in my cold bones, a father's
easily forgotten friendship for his son.

from **This Far North**

Penance

And still they live in unforgiven places,
on the sides of arthritic hills,
where low walls hide the sea and the sea
hides the dead, though the dead still whisper
in their silent graves, "I'm cold, I'm cold."

Enough bog here to stoke the fires of Hell,
and stones so many you'd think they grew
in the soil. Though nothing ever grows.
God knows there was more wood on Calvary.

This morning, on a high road beyond Cleggan,
I passed the ruins of a deserted cottage,
and a ruined cottage that looked deserted,
only a man eyed me. I asked where the road went?
"To the end," he said, "the end." Then shuffled off.

Preferences

I am fond of bicycles;
there is a great peace
in the shape of a wheel.

I like the way leaves
bend away from the sun
back toward the earth -
aware of the withering to come.

I like hills, rivers,
seas, woods.
I love the feel of stone
and the colour of grass.

And yet there are days
I drink for Ireland.

I am fond of books,
though not as fond as I used to be,
too many years in the woods
has turned my mind to heather and moss,
the occasional bluebell.

But I still like cigarettes
and Dylan songs,
favourite line - *I'm just whisperin'
to myself so I can't pretend that I don't know.*

I love women.
I love the poetry of Akhmatova.
I love the full moon, its white host
against the black body of the sky.

And yet there are days
I drink for Ireland.

I like hands,
fingers in particular.
I love the shape of lips.
I love the way one testicle
hangs lower than the other,
typical of life's imbalance.

I love tea on cold November mornings.
And for some reason I've never
understood, I love islands
and all they encircle.
I love the pure poetry of Beckett.

I am gazing out the window
at three small islands
and two trawlers
ploughing out to sea.
It is the last day of April.
The sea is smooth as a feather.

But I prefer
when it goes berserk
like a salty drunk
and rages against Ireland.

The Dreaming

> *A man who has lost his dream*
> *has lost his way.*
>
> —Aboriginal saying

If you stray from this road
you will be dead in a day.
If I had strayed I'd have
sung me a river and be tucked
in a hollow by nightfall.
I was the land and the land was me.

My world was sleeping until
my father dreamt the turtle
and the lizard. In his dream
I walked naked out of a lake
over the land towards the sea,
warmed always by the sun I sang.

Only at night I lit my fire
and painted my body,
following the lines of my bones
until I was a skeleton
dancing with the dead,
frightening away all evil.

And I kept it at bay
since the dawn of my dream,
until you came in disguise,
like me but not like me.
Your eyes stole my dream.
Your tongue my song.

But you have no voice for singing
and you sleep too unsettled to dream.
Your needs and your thoughts imprison you.
You have the cold embrace of a stranger.
Even your God has banished you naked.
I pity you and you think you pity me.

When Sometimes All I Can Imagine Are Hands

There is a winter within me,
a place so cold, so covered in snow,
I rarely go there. But sometimes,
when all I can imagine are hands,
when trees in the forest
look like they're made of wood,
then I know it's time
to take my photograph of Akhmatova
and sling it in a bag with socks and scarves.
My neighbours must think it strange
to see me strapping on my snowshoes,
to hear me roar at the huskies
as I untangle the harness.
But when all you can imagine are hands
it's best to give a little wave
and move out into the whiteness.

Unveiling

This could be Tuscany,
but for the rain, the mist,
and the hundreds of stone walls;
yesterday, as I clambered over one,
the whole lot came tumbling down on me.

You are gone only three days
and already I'm bruised inside and out.

I miss your hands and their unveiling.

They have begun a dig on Mooghaun Hill.
Three feet down the earth has revealed
the remains of an ancient hut,
its door, like ours,
facing away from the wind.

Hard to imagine that three feet
of leaves and dust have fallen
since someone last stood
in that doorway
waiting, as I do now, for the mountains
to define the shape and route of a woman.

Love, when you are home,
I will close this door
and though a thousand years of history
and a billion waning stars
are all around us,
we will sleep,
closer than feathers,
the breath of a kiss between us.

Archaeologists, digging for years,
might discover
that our house was here,
and our door faced away from the wind.
But what would they know
of the colour of your eyes,
how they darken in November?

The Dowser And The Child

When you were leaving
I always asked if you'd
brought an umbrella;
you made me think of rain
upon the hills. All our lives

there was a steady drizzle between us;
the sound of water in the distance.
Your hands, your eyes
dowsed over me, as if you
could divine things deep within me.

It seemed to me you moved beneath
a grey cloud. I remember,
even on sunny days, you wore
a great wide hat, your eyes
in darkness under the cool verandah.

Some days you were a passing shower.
Some days you were a snowflake.
Some days your tongue was a bolt
of lightning that sent me
scuttling under the kitchen table.

Hours I'd sit there, listening
to the thunder of your things
rolling in the distance.
Nights when the wind blew,
I could hear it moan in your room,

creaking the bed. If I opened your door,
you blew it shut with a shout.

Once when I was lost in the forest
at the back of our house, I followed
the cold wind that led home to you.

I ran down the path to embrace you,
but you stayed distant like all my
rainbows, and told me, and told me,
and told me, not to touch your
delicate colours with mucky hands.

I Am The Night-Watch

Years of living like a badger
have left me blind in daylight,
but in darkness I see things
with a clarity that haunts me.

To pass the hours I do yoga or T'ai-Chi.
Sometimes I just sit and meditate
or let my spirit astral travel
about the factory. I've crystals

buried to warn me of intruders;
theirs is a dark force against my light.
I try to stay hidden in shadows,
but I fear my aura gives me away,

it's silver grey like a badger's coat
and glows with the yellow of my chakra.
Vera, a theosophist, says our chakras
are like small tri-angular train stations

where elemental forces in the body
converge - little carriages of light
that should be realigned once a year
or immediately after a tragedy.

Thankfully I've less of those
since I began leaving my decisions
to readings from the I Ching
and the turning of Tarot cards.

Vera thinks my nervous compatibility
with the night may spring from the fact

that I was a badger in a past life.
But then she also thinks I was an owl.

I think I was a tree in the darkest
of forests that borrowed daylight
through the leaves. Because often,
when I least expect it, I find

I miss the warm sun on my face
and the many colours of grass,

Tea

> *The only sanity is a cup of tea.*
>
> -Gwendolyn Brooks

I

Sometimes I think I'm drowning
in all the tea I drink,
that someday I'll be found
floating, face up,
on the surface of myself.
A coroner's report will read
"died of tannin poisoning,
horrendous discolouration
and distortion of the vital organs,
brought on by imbibing a lethal
cocktail of incredible brews."
I began, like most,
with teas from India, China and Ceylon,
but moved quickly on to Camomile, Mu,
Luaka, Rosehip, Hibiscus, Lemon Grass,
Cherry Stems, Orange Flowers, Blueberry Leaves,
Blackberry Leaves, Rose Buds, Linden Flowers,
a veritable hothouse of horrid, herbal fusions.
Once, using the excuse that I was deeply in love,
I drank a fragrant mix of Passion Flowers,
Dandelion Leaves and Bancha Twigs.
I dream of a time when I can enjoy a Guinness
or something cool and clear as a gin and tonic.

11

My grandmother was also addicted.
The First World War caught her cold.
Tea rationed, she spent her days
recycling leaves or visiting friends.

With news of a second war
she moved my grandfather in
with the boys and filled his space
with boxes and boxes and boxes of tea.

For my grandmother
the First World War was hell,
but the second was a marvellous
bit of gossip to have with a brew.

The Coat

i.m. Osip Mandelstam

Are you a ghost, or a passing man,
for some reason I preserve your shade.

– Anna Akhmatova

The back of the chair now wears your coat,
it hangs as badly over its rickety frame
as it once did over yours. But on no other
chair does it look so well or remind me.

We were lame with the cold when they came
to arrest you; blue veins, like the rivers
of Europe, running over the backs of our hands.
Yet they stripped you down to the last word

and left me holding your empty coat.
I've replaced lost buttons, sewn the hem,
but I know you'll not be back for it
this winter nor the winter after.

To touch you now, I wrap your coat around me.
With my arms slipped into your arms,
and the belt pulled to the last notch,
I appear like your ghost returning.

Northern Haiku

    On an Antrim bog
a wall divides the wet land,
      planted in the past.

    Shot twice in the head.
Once in each astonished eye.
      History is blind.

    Over the dark Foyle
the bark of Kalashnikovs,
      an old Derry air.

    Punishment shooting.
Pleads remorse and forgiveness.
      Jeans gone at the knees.

Protestant prayers,
Popish prayers. Funerals.
We go the same way.

♣

A man out ploughing,
in one field he furrows from
Ireland to England.

♣

A blackbird's sweet song
lost in the wildness of hills -
prayer for the dead.

from Three Songs Of Home

Still Life

When I heard of the Tibetan
who made a clock
and then destroyed it
because it would be
yet another distraction,

I wondered was he troubled
by the ticking?
Was he worried he'd never
be quite sure whether to place it
on a shelf or by the bed?
Maybe he felt he'd always
be getting up to glance
at its slowly changing face
or to settle the hands.

So why did he make the clock?
Was it to see if time moved?
And then — suddenly —
at the first tick, it did,
and he began to wonder:
How long do I work?
What's it take to walk from one
end of the valley to the other?
Does day pass quicker than night?

I can see him now, that quiet man,
stepping away from the table,
taking a deep, slow breath,
as he lifts the hammer and swings
so the cogs, and the ticking,
and the time, vanish in a moment.

In Darjeeling

When the old Lama looked
curiously at me,
I thought it was to ask
why I hadn't touched
my yak-butter tea,
or what I thought the hands
of God might be holding
at this hour of the day.
Instead he asked,
in his faltering English,
why Americans found
the mountains so extraordinary.
"They're different," I said.
"Like me, they find them
mystical places."
"Oh!" he said,"and I thought
they were all circling fools.
When I pass them on the hills
they always say 'High!'
And 'Yes', I say, 'Very high',
and promise myself
to light a candle
for their circling souls."
"Father," I said, shaking my head,
"they say 'Hi!', and mean 'Hello!'".
He looked thoughtful for a moment.
"I think I've wasted
a thousand prayers
on a hundred kind greetings.
God must be laughing at Lama Doshi."

Prayer Guide

The beads Lobsang uses to count his prayers
are made from the bones of his father's hands.

Each time he comes to the end of a prayer, he slips
a piece of smooth white bone through his fingers

then begins his chant all over again;
his father's hand still guiding the way.

The Journey Home

i.m. Augustine Canavan

Some mornings
from my window
I can hear,
high up in the mountains,
the bell the monks ring
to call them to pray
for who they were,
who they are,
and who they will become,
on the journey home.

And some mornings
I join them in prayer,
imagining my own journey:
how far I've travelled
with so much baggage.
But the higher I've climbed
into the mountains,
the more I have discarded.

Let me tell you why I've come
to this ledge on a mountain,
this window on the snow-line:
it is to meet the ghost
who lives inside of me,
a man or woman I have not
seen for centuries, whose face,
whose voice, whose touch

I have forgotten,
but who knows my fear.
This soul who holds a bell for me,
that, at my last breath,
he'll ring to guide me home.

Now That I Am Almost Dead...

Now that I am almost dead
the ghosts in corridors
hold no fear for me.
I feel I know them.
They are teaching me to whisper,
to listen to others' conversation
as if I am not there. To leave
and enter rooms unnoticed; to fade.
And I can feel a ghost growing inside me.
What is hard is the loneliness,
the learning to live without dreams.

I walk the rooms at night
while others sleep,
knowing the skin that fits me now
will never fit so well again,
that my blue eyes will fade,
that my voice will soon be quiet.
And if I could wish,
it would be that when I die
your ghost still floats inside me,
and we haunt these rooms together,
or sleep eternally under a mountain,
the clay our blanket.

A Habitable Place

> 'There is no place on earth where death cannot
> find us — even if we constantly twist our heads
> in all directions as in a dubious and suspect land…'
>
> - Montaigne

Reach inside of me;
through the clay, through the forest,
deep into the clouds.
Open me; there's only sky,
one restless bird flying west.

All winter I dreamt
of a habitable place
to melt skin on skin;
lovers held warm as feathers,
cradled from the curse of ice.

The sky was empty
when I found the dead blackbird;
a sort of singing
gone forever with the wind.
Pray for us who have no wings.

Another evening
waiting for the light to die;
gone, almost grey now.
If I liken you to cloud;
there is no sky can hold you.

The grave still open,
all its crumbling earth still damp,
and my mother's breath,
cold as the trees in winter,
frozen on her last word 'home'.

No gift for talking,
yet she'd hear the dead whisper:
a sea of stories;
where they lived or where they died;
chatter of distant voices.

I wake in the night,
my mother's voice at my ear,
a river of sighs.
Darkness, the oddest country,
ghosts more living than the dead.

Must have been so old.
Must have heard other voices
and thought them the wind.
When I go down on my knees
the dust rises with my voice.

♣

When the dust settled
I was sat by the window
watching her dead hands;
colour was gone from her face,
as if her ghost frightened her.

♣

I have seen her ghost,
drawing itself on the road,
in search of its grave:
testing each six feet of earth,
the north wind cold in her eyes.

♣

And when the snow falls
the hills curl in on themselves
and the rivers freeze.
You open and close your door
as if birds are in the air.

♣

If death is a stone,
the haunted live in rivers,
gaze through fishes' eyes,
and though they cry in the night,
they are not blessed with voices.

The cross of evening
spreading out like a dark bird:
moon eyed, star feathered;
bright creature of this dark night —
you and I afraid of flight.

You told me of death,
said I'd climb to grasp its breath;
that I'd utter prayer;
that I'd carry my own soul
before I sank into earth.

Blue Bowl

for Paula Meehan

What she did
with all the blue bowls
I was never too sure,
but every time she went away
she brought one home.

When I visited,
I noticed she put
nothing in them,
and she did not
use them on the table.

I never asked her
about the bowls
for fear of offending
some tradition
I did not know about.

But this morning,
I mentioned them
to her husband,
Lobsang,
and he said,

"When she started
to gather them,
I too was intrigued.
So, one day,
I asked her.

Use them! she said,
*isn't each one filled
to the brim
with the memories
of a pilgrimage?*

She pointed to a bowl.
*That contains
the first days of spring,
and every step from here
to the monastery at Rongbuk.*

*And this, this tiny blue
bowl, is late autumn
on the road to Namche;
many icy days
and long dark nights."*

And did you find out
why they're always blue?
"Yes, but not from her.
On a pilgrimage of my own
I asked an old Lama.

She chooses a blue bowl
so it won't be out of place
with the others, or seem
somehow more important
when it's filled."

Lobsang's Last Wish

Lobsang loves the smell
of things. He says,
when you are dying,
it is the last of the senses to leave.

So, on that particular day,
he will fill the room
with all the wildflowers
that grow along the riverbank.

Then, when the other senses
are gone, when the eyes
are blind, when the room
is hushed, when the pain

is so great he won't
even remember
to remember
to pray,

in that darkness,
the smell of a yellow
petal might bring
him back long enough

to give thanks for such
small blessings,
and die a grateful
rather than a bitter man.

The Voyage

It is years since I last crossed
by boat to Ireland,
but tonight I am going home
over the waves.
The sky is filled with fading stars,
their light has travelled for a million years
and they are weary ; the last trace
of the light that left us here.

I'd promised to be in Dublin by summer,
but it is the first of November:
the first day of winter.
The decks are icy underfoot
and there is snow in the air. Behind me,
a man is asking a woman if she loves him?
It is far too cold for such great questions.
It is an Irish night, under an Irish sky.

And I am beginning to remember this voyage:
the beer, the songs, the cigarettes;
the asthmatic wheeze of the engine
as it lifts us over another mountainous wave.
It is all up hill to Ireland:
against the tide, against the wind,
against the dark and the cold.
The journey, preparing us for the land.

A Quiet House

Since I've moved to the hills
I've stopped sleeping naked,
but taken to planting flowers;
not just in the garden,
but in cooking-pots, buckets,
any old containers.
This year, when you return,
there will be laburnum, iris,
seven types of fuchsia,
to waken to each morning.
And I make this promise to you now:
I have done with travelling.
I am mending the wood
in the window, the tap at the sink.
I am letting the clocks run down.
This time, the house will whisper
when you sleep, and it will take, at least,
nine hours of moonlight to waken you.

from **What Darkness Covers**

Blind

Now when I call, she says,
"Step close and let me see you."
She lifts her fingers onto my face,
then up over my eyes so I go blind.

I smell the lavender on her hands,
the ash in the grate, cat smells, church smells,
turf and apple-mint. An apron hung to dry.
The smell of the yard on boots by the door.

And beyond the door, the weather:
rain and mist. Earth-smells:
cattle and woodburn. The dead leaves
at the dead end of the year. And all

through the wood, the whirling wind,
the open wing, eggshell and birdsong,
and mosses from the riverbank
smelling of frog and flick of fish tail.

Then, as she lifts her fingers
releasing my eyes back into the light,
"You're looking well," she says,
and asks for news of weather and the day.

Juliet Sleeping

Unused to a baby
in the house,
the grandmother
has emptied turf
from a creel
and filled it with
soft cotton sheets.
Now Juliet sleeps
in a wicker bed,
dreaming of moss.

"And not just moss,"
the grandmother says,
"but all of the woods,
the light and the half-light,
for it is late autumn
and this child is dreaming
the brown into her eyes."

Masterplan

God made today
as he will make tomorrow,
as he made yesterday.

He has been doing this,
year in, year out,
for as long as I can remember.

The only thing he changes
is the weather
and how he moves

the people under the clouds:
some he brings into the world,
some he takes away.

He works magic with flowers,
miracles with water,
sorcery with stars.

He does this and that
and hallelujahs,
and bucketfuls of sadness.

What he does with love
and hate is a *tour-de-force:*
in a moment he can

break or mend your heart.
He assures us in his book
he has a masterplan,

that every step is neatly mapped
from the sorrow of whale song,
to the shyness of the platypus.

But all I want from him
is to slow
the whole thing down

so I can at least appreciate
all the work he has put in,
covering up the cracks.

Still Life with Books

Most mornings I wake early
as if I have somewhere to go,
something to do. I potter
for an hour through books,
papers, photographs.

Then I sit by the window
for the rest of the day.

And if there is rain,
I fish for tears.
And if there is mist,
I sift for ghosts.
And if there is snow,
I chisel for stars.

In between
I pace the room
or watch the gate
for the comfort
of the postman. How
did I end up like this?

A watcher of skies
and fields that run to clouds;
a keeper of stillness,
a moonface at the window,
a love gone to darkness,
a still life with books.

Nude

She has been with me all winter.
I cannot say I hate her
for when I was young
I loved everything about her.
There were nights
I could have died for her.
Now there's an awful
pattern to our lives.

She arrives late September
carrying sacks of old books,
and pinned to her dress
or tied in her hair,
or buried in the folds
of her skin,
are those few new poems
I have waited all summer to hear.

But each year her price
goes a little higher
and I grow weary.
Often she undresses
to the bone:
peeling her skin,
folding the wrinkled
hide over the bed
where she sups and stares.

Often she strips me too,
planting the tips
of her fingers
like roots in my eyes,
or pushing her tongue
deep into my mouth.
Bare. Naked. Nude —
unless you've ever
served her,
felt her cunning
on your lips,
you'll never know
the meaning of the word.

And yet,
one of these mornings
I'll find her
standing in the kitchen
dressed for the road,
coat, hat, scarf,
bags tied with string,
and I'll be on my knees
begging her to stay.

What Darkness Covers

Because I cannot sleep
and you are far away,
this dishevelled bed
holds no dreams,
and blankets and darkness
cover only emptiness.
I look where you should be
but you are utterly gone.
I lie remembering.

My grandmother used to say
the dead love this time of year,
the nights so long
they walk amongst us whispering.
This morning I found
footprints on the path,
tears on every leaf.
Listen, is that a door opening
or a door closing?

Old Italians used to say
the most beautiful sculpture
Michelangelo ever made
was a snowman
in the Boboli Gardens:
a male nude chiselled out of ice,
you could see where his soul
was held. He turned all to tears
and was washed away.

I do this all the time,
try to hold on.
Sometimes I feel
I am the last leaf on the tree,
and there will be no rest
until I fall. So I say —
Let everything that falls, fall,
beginning with tired love
and ending in the old way:

the eyes still,
the breath gone,
all quiet until
the earth's rain falls.

Baffled

Like you, I have spent
most of my life baffled.
No sooner does the light
dawn than it's dark again.
There are times I wonder
why I get out of bed
to traipse the streets
like a familiar ghost
heading for the fruit market.
How can bananas
become somebody's life?

And before this,
when I lived in the
grave-diggers cottage,
she said my skin
always smelt of the dead.
Six feet down,
level with their bones,
I could hear them sighing.
Mid-winter, I'd swear
their eyes were watching.
Fewer died over Christmas,
most panted on until
the new year, gave
out crossing the line.
*What did you get
for Christmas? A grave.*

The Parish Priest
would call down
"Make sure you

square the edges.
Nothing settles out
a life better than
a smooth descent."
His own went as easily
as the tide turning.
I can still remember
my surprise at how
upset she was. As they
lowered the coffin
she began to cry.
I thought at first
it was a seagull.

Living close to the shore
they were always on at me
to go to sea. But though
I loved an old dip, the sea
is something else
that has always baffled me:
its goes up, it goes down.
It comes in, it goes out,
like a drunk's friendship
with his favourite bar.
And then for no reason
other than a freshening breeze
or a scrap of cloud,
it flies into a rage
and spits stones.
Bad weather, and the boats
could be tied up for weeks.
If you want me, I'll be in the bar.

Strange that when you are young
she lies before you
like a floozie.
You suck and swallow
suck and swallow
until thirty years later
you stare across
the table at the shadow
keeping you company
and say, *"One of these days
I must give this up."*
He laughs and gets in
another round
and the world spins on...

We live for what we love
and wait for death.
Surely love and death
are the two great shrines
to the bewildered.
I am a disciple of one
heading towards the other,
bothered that life
is not a tightrope
along which we edge
in our own creaky fashion,
but something tossed away
by a famished god,
a banana skin awaiting
the heel of another
hapless pilgrim.

Jimmy

For who can bear to feel himself forgotten.
W.H Auden

That old soldier,
he still comes round
every odd Tuesday afternoon.
He brings a glass eye,
a useless arm,
and all the war
that lingers on his skin;
a withered heart.
and yet, Jimmy
has the gentlest soul
I've ever known;
it's just he could never
climb out of the trench
they left him in.

These days he shuffles
when he walks
and his good hand shakes:
dampness gone to the bone.
Last night,
stroking my breasts,
he said the tips of my nipples
were smooth as bullets.
Then the air went silent,
as if we were waiting
for shells to fall,
I looked at him
sprawled naked,
a wounded man.

And I saw tears,
saw the glass-eye
like a sheet of ice
covering a flood.

Lemon Tree

Christmas in Melbourne,
and there is a lemon tree
at the back of the house.

In all my life I could not
use so many lemons:
all those coughs and colds,

all those gin and tonics,
all those dreary salads,
all that sweet bitterness.

It is so hot here now
I have spent all afternoon
in its sandy shade

imagining you here,
dressed only in an open kimono,
the wind revealing you

to me at her will
as I sip sweet tea,
the little moons of lemon,

like this
abandoned love,
bitter to the end.

Small Interior

> *If you wandered through a poet's*
> *brain you would not see poetic*
> *thoughts there.*
>
> \- Gwen Harwood

The room I write in has an oak door, a wooden floor,
a well of book shelves, a window and a table where I sit
with my back to the light. On the walls around me
are the postcards, small greetings from wandering souls.
A quick glance and I see Puccini, Beckett, a study of a
naked woman posing on a chair. There are paintings by
Picasso, Gauguin, Bacon, Mattise; Chagall's wedding is
pinned up and Schiele's *Reclining Woman,* I found her in
the V&A.

Wish you were here!

I've one, two, three, four nudes by Lucian Freud;
cards from London's New Tate. And from Paul in
Liverpool, not the Beatles or the Mersey, but lots of
Edward Hopper: late-night bars where men in coats sip
bourbon — any one of them could be Dylan Thomas,
circa 1953. And he's up there too, painted by Augustus
John, the big man who painted the poet's wife.
She used to say he took her on the studio floor.

Everything's so cheap!

There's a card from Istanbul, a map of the old city —
wouldn't that be Byzantium? There's a photo of me
standing by the Bosphorus taken the day I took a taxi
from Asia to Europe. And there's a great photo of you
naked on a beach in Australia reading Judith Wright's
poems, the ocean behind you so blue.

Weather's lovely!

♣

There are Tibetan mandalas beside irreverent cartoons.
There are invitations to launches, invitations to tea,
rejections, receipts, notes, bills. And dotted between
them is a sprinkling of islands: the Blaskets, the
Orkneys, the Shetlands, Crete, Tasmania, Sicily.
How are they formed? Does the earth rise or the water
recede? Someone told me that Everest was once at the
bottom of the ocean, and climbers close to the top
often find shells. I wonder do they still hold the sound
of the sea?

The beach is beautiful!

♣

Only two of the cards are in black and white: Bob
Dylan travellin' through Balbriggan station on his way
to play Belfast in the summer of '65 and a John
Minihan photo of a duffel-coated Beckett drinking
coffee, smoking a cheroot and waiting for someone.
Was he ever photographed in summer? Minihan has
frozen him forever in a polo-neck and duffle.

I'm practically naked all day!

This morning a card arrived from Jack in Berlin, another nude: a German woman photographed in 1935. I wonder how she fared in the war? I'll put her up there close to the ceiling, out of harm's way, between a poster by the Mexican painter Alfonso Lopez Monreal and a picture of a Cistercian monastery at Tarrawarra, in the Yarra valley, about forty miles outside Melbourne. My uncle Paul was a monk there; I got it when I visited the monastery last year.

So peaceful and quiet!

A spring morning, the monks brought me out to the small graveyard where Paul is buried under a simple iron cross. They showed me the church where he prayed, the shed where he mended things; sat me in his old truck and sang the first verse of his favourite song. They said he sang it when he drove the sheep to the market in Melbourne, Gene Autry's *South of the Border Down Mexico Way*. N.D.A was printed on the truck's door and when the farmers or the bushmen asked him what it stood for, he'd declare "No dames allowed!".

Still on my own!

Each card is a dream filter, a small bell that chimes in my soul. If I had to choose one for Desert Island Discs, I'd choose the nude of you on that beach in Australia. But I suppose that would be like taking Shakespeare or the Bible. So I'd go with either Billie Whitelaw in *Happy Days* or William Orpen's *Sunlight*.

It's pretty as a picture here!

♣

Apart from this morning's post, my latest acquisitions are *The Death of Culture* by the American model and photographer Lee Miller, and an unforgettable photograph of her soaking in Hitler's bath during the last days of war. I bought them in Edinburgh. I pinned them either side of Gary Snyder's "What You Should Know To Be A Poet". I love that poem, it's great last line: "real danger. gambles. and the edge of death".

I could happily die here!

♣

Looking round my room I sometimes think that this is what it must be like inside my head: a higgle of postcards held up by ghosts, a thousand images falling like rain, a patchwork, a shadowland of ifs and buts. Of who is she? And who is he? And when and where was that? And then, when I close my eyes to look more closely there is always only the same small black and white self-portrait of me; it's untitled, but I call it:

Nude, in small interior.

Two Poems After Paintings by Lucian Freud.

Big

It wasn't that I was always this big.
It wasn't that at four years of age
I began eating only doughnuts.

It's something in me:
an old ache, not heartache,
but something like neglect.

The year would turn
and every summer
I'd be bigger than before.

And then your man
stopped me in the street
saying he'd like to paint me, nude.

Pervert, I thought,
and so old
with mean eyes,

skinny as a whippet.
I asked him to leave me alone
and take himself back to the home.

But a week later, he called to my hatch —
I'm a benefit supervisor —
with photos of his work.

They were nothing like I'd seen
before: men and women naked
but dressed; living in their skin.

Six months I sat for him
in his studio
on the Marylebone Road.

Now I'm up on the wall
in the New Tate,
for everyone to see.

When I go to see myself
people always point
and the guard winks.

I sometimes wonder
what my mother
would have made of me.

I suppose she wouldn't
have minced her words.
But I think, naked

I look glorious.
Look at me:
I look like a woman

taking a bath without water.
A saint burning without flames.
A bird opening its wings.

I look through a painter's eyes.
I look like I never looked before,
and yet, exactly the same.

Naked Girl With Egg

Up to this he always painted me
as just a naked model upon a sheet.

A while ago he began adding
two fried eggs (sunny side up).

I thought he was enjoying a joke;
the eggs so similar to my breasts.

As he painted it dawned on me,
the eggs were my ovaries;

all I meant to him
was the cold white dish.

The Olympians

Next up are the poets.
This was never going
to be a glorious race
but, after the pandemonium
of the heats,
let's at least make sure
they're all facing the same way.

Running in lane one
in anonymous and fragments,
with a withered arm
and halt leg,
it's the Greek beauty Sappho,
all sandy smiles
and dark brown eyes,
its rumoured
she moves like the wind

Beside her, in lane two,
with the haiku -
seventeen steps
of grace and precision -
its the butterfly
of the short line,
representing Japan,
the little man, Basho.

In three with the sonnet
is William Shakespeare,
his run will depend
on impeccable rhythm,
on getting it all to flow.

Though a shadow is cast
over his selection
with Percy Shelley,
William Wordsworth,
Samuel Coleridge
and George Gordon, Lord Byron
all testing positive for opiates.

In lane four
with the villanelle
its the Welshman Dylan Thomas:
after a lifetime of injuries
and unfulfilled promise —
it's marvellous to see him
finally up on his feet.

In the middle of the field,
standing out like a king,
is the long-distance legend,
blind Homer from Greece.
Kit Smart was a contender, but
he never turned up for the race.

Beside him,
crammed into six,
are Dante —
the Italian wizard,
the antelope of terza rima —
and a couple of farm boys,
Frost and Heaney.
I've seen them in practise,
they move with deceptive ease.

In lane seven, in the four
by four hundred relay
it's the Russian champions —
they pass the baton
with silk-like grace —
Pasternak to Tsvetayeva,
Tsvetayeva to Mandelstam,
Mandelstam to Akhmatova.
She brings it home
with tremendous power
and gritty determination.

Out in lane eight,
going round the bend,
there's an army of poets.
I recognise at least a hundred
faces preparing for the start.

And then,
not with a shot
or a shout,
but with a collective sigh,
they're off.

It is poetry in motion,
like something out of Brueghel
the stillness is absolute,
for no one has moved.

They have closed their eyes
and are imagining
the wind on the faces,

the sweat on the brow
the pain in the chest
the ache in the hearts
the hardship
the loneliness,
the grief,
that has brought them to this.

Some are already
closing on the line.
Others will take
hours, days, weeks months.
Some will still be running
when the crowds are gone
when the lights are off
when the stadium's closed

And some will
never make it home:
their words, their faces,
their lives forgotten.
They will turn to dust
where they fall.
The earth takes back
what it gives away -
the lanes run on forever.

Another Room

This was our room,
it has four walls,
I counted them
when you left:

The one with the door,
the one with our pictures,
the one with the window,
the one with our bed.

But now, to put away the memory
of how your hands, your mouth
turned my skin into electricity,
I have taken myself away.

I have moved to another room.
It too has four walls,
but the door opens to the other side,
and there are no pictures of you.

And in the dark,
when I bury your ghost,
the memory of your touch
goes out with the light.

Now Winter's Over

I've been told this winter's nearly over,
so I'd like to give thanks to you, O Lord,
and if not to you, than to whoever
led me through; for someone
kept me still under tumbling skies,
warm even on the darkest days.

Now, as she retreats, I watch her fold
her blanket of leaves in the field,
load her wagon with boxes of frost,
sheaves of ice, rolls of mist, barrels of rain.

Her last act will be
disposing of her enemies
caught like lambs in the briars —
the crows will pluck out their eyes.

From an open window
I'll watch green leaves
lick the blood from raindrops,
coax the life out of sunbeams,

suck till the smell of spring fills the air:
the cries of children in streets
the crackle of yellow crocuses
the eyes of leaves opening on trees.

If it weren't for the rest
of this dishevelled world,
I'd almost dare to say
I am happy to be alive.

Currach

This is my boat.
I made it
with my own hands.
I took salt
from a bitter wind,
hair from
a horse's mane,
thread from
a woman's blouse.

Three stories
my father told me.
The sideways look
my mother has
when she is
curious and alone.
Her silent prayers.
A few rusty nails
from the kitchen door.

Three views of the island:
one in mist, one in rain,
one rocking in a drunken sea.
No flowers.
My people
had no love of leaves,
they saw boats in trees;
now the boats are gone
and the hills are bare.

At night, I sowed
curses into the oars,
rubbed fish oil
into the wood,
for I knew the journey
that lay ahead.
My people's story
was written on water.
Most of it is washed away.

My grandfather
knew the tale
but he'd not tell it.
His ghost sits
in the stern
saying:
*"The future
is a steady course,
row strongly."*

The Boat

Now that I have come this far there is no
        turning back.
And yet, what if there is nothing at the end
        of the track?

What if there is only more rock and sea?
        What if when
you open your eyes there's still the interminable
        grey rain?

Will you take it out on me? Or will you say,
        let us make our bed here.
Winter approaches and we need food
        and shelter.

For even in this emptiness we have each other.
        We are from the same mould,
close as body and soul, feather and air, fish
        and water, rain and wind.

And brushing the hair from your face, will you
        take my hand and place it on
your breast saying: How were you to know
        the boats would leave so soon?

How were you to know the boats were here at all?
        So, let me settle.
Cities have been built by men like you,
        waiting for the boat home.

from **The Magical Book of Winter Cures**

The Cure For A Broken Heart

And this is the first of the healing cures,
the oldest remedy, the most often used,
it is of course for the broken hearted.
They come trailing clouds of dust,
their faces wet with tears. No excuses,
just an emptiness about them.
Beyond worry. The journey over.
They open their mouths and sip
like sinners seeking redemption;
then enter the darkness that I am.
In this room without walls, they bolt
the door, lie down and wait for the cure
to wash it all away: white as the winter sky.
A shower of hair over a pillow, a last memory.

The potion:

Seven days when no one calls.
Seven nights when nothing stirs.
Seven walks in the rain.
Seven ferocious prayers.
Seven gentle curses.
Seven lakes to swim in.
Seven woods to wander in.
Seven axes to cut away the wood.
Seven blades to cut away the skin.
Seven beds to toss in.

Seven master plans.
Seven panic attacks.
Seven circles of the asylum.
Seven hairs from the pillow.
Seven howls of rage.
Seven on seven on
Seven hours staring out the window
Seven currachs ready for the voyage.
Seven bags of books
Seven paintings.
Seven empty rooms.
Seven sleep filled nights.
Seven songs of thanks.

How to mix this cure,
where best to take it
depends on who you are.
I wonder if everything's here -
at its terrible cost,
I'd hate to think anything's lost.

Cure For Loneliness

This is an old Russian cure,
better than a cup of tea,
more reliable than pills.
It was first formulated
by Leo Tolstoy in the
long winter of 1869.
A complex potion,
the recipe runs to 1,144 pages,
too long to put down here,
but you'll find it on the creaking
shelves of any library
under the heading *War and Peace*.

I suggest you take it
late at night,
beside an open fire,
with a map of old Russia
and a bottle of red wine.
I tried it myself
and it worked fine for me:
all the ghosts in my head
gathered round to hear
the tale of love and loss.

You could also try
some very old remedies
by Homer or Catullus,
or powerful ones
by Dante or Shakespeare,
or witches brews
by Sappho or Tsvetayeva,
or complex Irish potions

by Messrs Joyce and Beckett.
Their cures hold a mirror up
to your soul — they work
incredibly well, though
I have found them addictive,
and the Beckett repeats
at odd times of the night.

These days
there is a whole
new range of panaceas:
heal-alls, cure-alls,
some are like fire,
others like ice, but
none have been
tested by time.
However,
I do recommend,
for those darkest days,
the small healing potions
by Michael Hartnett.